# ANIMAL LIFE STORIES
# THE FOX

Published in 1988 by Warwick Press,
387 Park Avenue South, New York, N.Y. 10016.
First published in this edition by
Kingfisher Books, 1988. Some of the illustrations
in this book are taken from the First Look
at Nature series.

6 5 4 3 2 1

Printed in Spain

Library of Congress Catalog Card No. 87-51623
ISBN 0-531-19040-4

# ANIMAL LIFE STORIES

# THE FOX

By Angela Royston
Illustrated by Bernard Robinson

**Warwick Press**
**New York/London/Toronto/Sydney**
**1988**

The young fox curls up with her bushy tail wrapped around her nose and falls asleep. Two days ago she left the woods where she had lived with her mother and the other cubs. She has traveled a long way since then and now she is tired.

The fox wakes in the evening. It is time to continue her journey, but first she must eat. She smells chickens at a farm nearby and waits until it is dark. Then she creeps through a gap in the wire. The hens in the hen house cluck with fear and wake a hen sleeping on the roof. It flaps and the fox pounces and kills it.

When she has eaten, the fox runs on until daybreak. Then she stops in a wood, too tired to go any farther. Luckily she finds a tunnel with a grassy hollow in it, but as she settles down to sleep she hears a scuffling noise. The badger who made the underground home is coming back. The fox runs away and sleeps under a hawthorn bush instead.

That night the fox explores the wood. It smells of rabbits and mice. But the smell she notices most is the scent of other foxes. She follows these scent trails and decides to make her home in the wood.

There are plenty of blackberries, beetles, and snails for the fox to eat, and she hunts frogs and bigger prey. One night she finds a hedgehog but can't unroll the prickly animal and hurts her paw.

Summer passes and the fox must find an earth for the cold winter months. She chooses an old fox hole, but first clears out the rubbish left by the last fox.

The fox walks round and round the area near her earth so that she can leave her scent on trees and grass. She wants other foxes to know she is there.

Now that she has a comfortable home the vixen wants
a mate. At night she wails and barks, calling to the
male foxes who live nearby.

After some nights a dog-fox hears her and hurries to answer her calls. Every night they play together in mock battles and soon they mate.

Now it is deep winter and food is hard to find. The fox has to be clever and brave. She steals ducks from a farm and even attacks deer twice her size.

Seven weeks after she mated the vixen's cubs are born. The cubs curl up close to her to keep warm. She stays close to her cubs, feeding them with her milk and washing them while her mate brings her food.

When spring arrives the cubs are nearly a month old. One evening they leave the earth for the first time. The vixen watches out for danger as the cubs play together in the open air. They chase flies and feathers blowing in the wind. They pounce on each other and on their mother's tail, and fight for bones.

When they are two months old the cubs are big enough to go hunting with their mother. They look for birds' nests and steal the eggs. They learn to pounce on their prey instead of snapping at it, and soon they can catch rabbits, voles, and mice, too.

Summer arrives and the vixen is tired from looking after her family. She needs to rest before winter comes. One by one, the cubs leave their mother and the wood and set out to find their own place to live.

## More about Foxes

There are twelve different kinds of foxes living in different parts of the world. The white Arctic fox lives in the coldest northern lands while the little sandy-colored fennec fox lives in the desert. The fox in this story is a red fox. Red foxes live in many countries. Usually they live in woods and moorlands where they can move into old holes dug by other creatures.

As well as living in other animals' homes, foxes do not always kill their own food. They are quite happy to eat whatever food they can find. For this reason, some foxes now live on the edges of towns or along railway lines where they can raid nearby garbage cans for food.

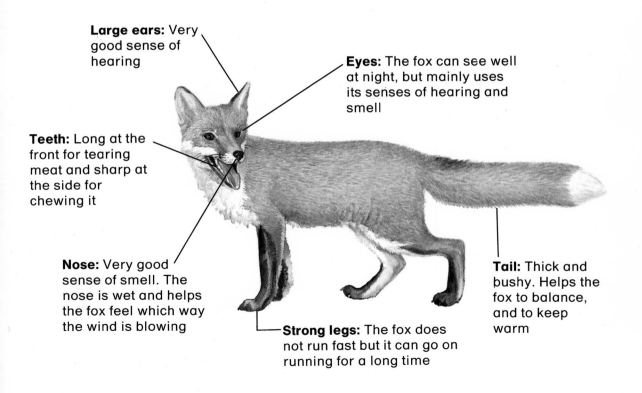

**Large ears:** Very good sense of hearing

**Eyes:** The fox can see well at night, but mainly uses its senses of hearing and smell

**Teeth:** Long at the front for tearing meat and sharp at the side for chewing it

**Nose:** Very good sense of smell. The nose is wet and helps the fox feel which way the wind is blowing

**Strong legs:** The fox does not run fast but it can go on running for a long time

**Tail:** Thick and bushy. Helps the fox to balance, and to keep warm

# Some Special Words

**Brush** A fox's tail is called a brush. When the fox goes to sleep it curls up and wraps its tail around itself like a warm scarf.

**Cub** A young fox.

**Den** In summer, foxes have no particular home. They sleep anywhere, in dens which they make in clumps of bushes, in ditches, or among rocks.

**Dog-fox** A male fox.

**Earth** In winter foxes find an earth, an underground home. They never make their own, but take over a rabbit burrow or a badger's home, or find an empty space underneath rocks or even under a garden shed.

**Mock battle** Fox cubs play at fighting, which helps them learn the skills they need for hunting.

**Vixen** A female fox.